LIFE LESSONS
FROM MY DOG

LIFE LESSONS FROM MY DOG

PATRICIA BUDD KEPLER

Library of Congress Control Number:		2006909372
ISBN 10:	Softcover	1-4257-3998-9
ISBN 13:	Softcover	978-1-4257-3998-0

This book was printed in the United States of America.

To order additional copies of this book, contact:

Xlibris Corporation

1-888-795-4274

www.Xlibris.com

Orders@Xlibris.com

36739

Contents

Introduction 9

Why A Dog? The Home Coming 13

Joy For Life 19

Getting It: The Basics of Togetherness 25

Appearance and Essence 29

My Trouble With Alpha Dogs 34

Widening The Circle 41

Getting Through The Hard Times 51

Leave It! 57

Communication: The Language of the Heart 65

Real Change 73

Happy Birthday 77

Dedication

This book is dedicated to the faithful pets who have enriched our lives through the years: Terpsichore, Sam, Midnight, Max, Cochise, Particle, Hailey, Nigel, Liza, and **Miranda**.

With gratitude to my family for sharing their lives with these animal companions when they were growing up, and with appreciation for Harold and Fran Budd for their true love of animals.

Special thanks to Thomas F. Kepler for copy editing this book, to "Canine University®" of Malden Massachusetts for their educational contribution, and to the folks at Xlibris for getting it into print.

INTRODUCTION

WHEN ONE OF my granddaughters was learning to read, she occasionally read words backwards. Dog and God were interchangeable.

Then I got a dog. Very subtly, and at first almost unconsciously, I began to reflect on my relationship to God and my self-understanding through observing my interactions with my dog. I remembered my granddaughter's word reversal. I certainly won't confuse God and Dog, but maybe I can learn something about God through my relationship with my dog.

Didn't the Psalmist proclaim the ways in which all nature praises God, who is manifest in all creation?

We have always understood God through experience as well as through the written word. Theology is relational, exploring the interconnectedness of all things. Why can't we learn something about God through nature, even through a dog's nature, and about ourselves through our relationship with the canine species?

I began to put some of my meandering thoughts down on paper: God/Dog – what has my granddaughter allowed me to stumble upon?

Clearly, what follows is a one-sided reflection. My dog can't speak for herself; you are seeing her and our relationship through my eyes. I hope I get it right from her perspective some of the time. However, she doesn't seem to care about what I put on paper. What really matters to her is that I read her correctly, correctly enough to meet her needs and appreciate her trying to understand and please me. The desired end result for both of us is a harmonious and fulfilling relationship, and a hospitable, interesting connection with the rest of the world.

From the beginning, I know that simple things are going to matter. We will have to live by certain rules of behavior. We will have to try to communicate across our species divide. We will have to negotiate our expectations of one another. In other words, we will have to work at being together in exchange for happiness.

What follow are some reflections on how my relationship with another form of animal life sometimes opens a window on my relationship with God, a form of Spirit life, and thereby opens a window on myself.

WHY A DOG?
THE HOME COMING

H AVING A DOG was my idea. My husband was less than enthusiastic. For my sake, he finally agreed to our getting one with the understanding that this was to be my dog and I was to take care of her!

For months I read newspaper ads and books. I watched videos and scrutinized every dog I came across. I bored friends and family alike with my preoccupation with a DOG. We had gotten dogs from shelters in the past and loved every one of them, so that was the first place we looked. But there were no available dogs in the shelters near us at that time. I settled on getting a Wheaten Terrier, but when I found out how expensive they were, they fell from the list. I had to reassess my options and choices.

Then I saw an ad in the paper for Standard Poodles. We went to visit them in a private home and fell in love. We chose our dog out of a litter of nine, but had to wait until she was eight weeks old before we could pick her up. Summer vacation out of state turned eight weeks into nine. Then finally, the day came to pick up our puppy.

Two of our grandchildren came along on the big day. We loaded ourselves into the car and made the hour-long drive to our destination in great anticipation. I was prepared with a blanket to hold her in and paper towels in case she threw up. The girls had a toy for her.

The teenager who had helped care for her met us at the door with a friend, and a puppy in her arms. Our puppy! We were all very excited. My husband held our dog while I took a picture to record this important day.

Then came the ride home. Puppy was in my lap, wiggling and yelping all the way. She kept trying to climb over my shoulder to get into the back seat with the girls. But she did not throw up. A good sign, since we like to travel.

Now there was no turning back. The dog is ours, and with two grandchildren as accomplices, we have added a new member to our family. We try to settle her in and settle ourselves down. One of the girls draws a picture of herself and the dog in honor of the day.

Our lives are now intertwined with this new squirmy form of life. Until the last two years, a dog has always been part of our household. So having a dog in our lives is not new. But this dog is new and will be herself, different from all the others. And she comes to me when I am in a new place in my life.

I think about the God/Dog connection. God is not someone you bring home like a puppy. God is always there, sometimes in the background, sometimes at the center. But I remember a picture from my childhood Sunday-School lessons: Jesus is standing at the door and knocking. God may be always there, but we were told that we either invite God in or we don't.

As an adult I know that faith can be a complicated matter. Sometimes we are ambivalent about the whole matter of religion and there is no simple, God in or God out. God comes when we expect it least, and can seem to be absent when we most want God to be near. Still, there is the image of God as the hound of heaven, pursuing us. That is comforting.

Do I really want a puppy? Always? I am sure there will be times when my enthusiasm wanes.

Just like my passion for my relationship to God. Deep down, I know that God has always been part of my life. As I grow older, there is something different about my experience of God. I can let my preconceived notions go. I want to be real and I want God to be real, authentic. Transparent . . . like our puppy.

I look at the puppy. She is going to be who she is and we are going to have to negotiate life together.

I mentioned the fact that I am in a new stage of my life. I have just left my last full time paid work. People are puzzled about why I want a dog at this point in my life when I could be most completely free.

There are several ways to look at freedom.

One possibility is that I wanted a dog because I could not stand the thought of freedom. I wanted to be tied down. I must be suffering from the "empty nest" syndrome. Another possibility is that I thought a dog would give me more freedom of spirit, and more vitality. Maybe I weighed the occasional limitations of having a dog against the daily pleasures and companionship and decided that giving up a little freedom was acceptable.

I confess to having stereotypical images in my head of a happy family that always includes a dog resting peacefully by the fireplace. This dog would be my animal companion, my alter ego, my muse. And we don't have a fireplace in our house, but even if we did, we got a high energy dog who wouldn't spend her days resting there!

But there was something else, too. My father had died suddenly and much too soon, before we could say good-bye and before he could write the book he had planned to write on Real Estate Law. I reached the age at which he had died, praying for more time with my family and enough years to fulfill his dream of writing a book – maybe even books.

I am not afraid to die. I am just not ready. I have so much to live for. I love life, even with all its problems, complications, and occasional disappointments. I think I saw a dog as a visible symbol of my true longing for longevity, silly as that sounds. A big dog lives for ten years. If I had a dog around to care for, then I would have to live at least ten years. She would be a life-giving force at this stage of life. While God is my ultimate salvation, the dog would be a source of immediate satisfaction. She would be a live-in reminder of all the other reasons I have for living.

Too often in the past when I thought about God, it was in terms of everlasting life, life after death. Now, more than ever, I want the emphasis of my religion to be on life before death. I need my relationship with God to be an affirmation of all that is good and beautiful in this world. I want to enjoy God, and leave the unknown in God's hands.

There is scientific evidence that animals can improve the quality of life for older people. People bring animals into nursing homes. My mother enjoyed her dog so much in the last years of her life that when her dog died, we thought she would too. (We thank God she didn't!)

For longevity there is medicine, meditation, diet, exercise, genes, familial support, and a positive spirit. Add to my list, my dog and my God. I don't really want to place the burden of keeping me alive on my new dog. But she doesn't care. As for God, God is there in life and death.

For whatever reason (or maybe for no discernible reason), I wanted and got a dog. Now I live with her and with myself living with her. And as I write, she is trying to get me to play with her, rubbing her messy bone up against my arm. I tell her to get lost, but I am glad she is around. She makes me smile.

"Behold, I make all things new." I have a banner with those words embroidered on it by a dear colleague I worked with during our nation's Bicentennial, Sister Concilia Moran, a Sister of Mercy like my cousin Rosemary. Dog is new, new to the world and new in my life.

JOY FOR LIFE

WHEN THE WINTER sets in, I brace myself for retrenchment and mild depression: less light, a colder house, fewer warm rooms, the closing off of porches, and reduced physical activity.

Snow came early this year. I know snow. I have seen hundreds of snowstorms and helped shovel many paths. But my dog had never seen snow. She was absolutely delighted by the white stuff. She ran through it and rolled in it. She ate it and sniffed it and lifted her head to greet the falling snowflakes.

She set something in me free. It was as if I was seeing snow for the first time too, an occasion for fun and frolic. The beauty of fresh-fallen snow thrilled me. I caught my dog's delight. Her sheer joy was in her whole body. She was having an in-body experience.

She loved it. How could I not go along? She took me back to the days when our children were young and excited by snow, and to my own childhood.

The other day, after playing in the yard, she lay down right in the middle of the snow. She almost matched it . . . but she was a little off-color, a kind of cream hue against the sheer white. I wondered how she could do that. I would love to be as at-home in the elements as she was.

She loved the autumn too. She caught the falling leaves in her mouth. She romped in the piles of leaves we had raked, and with the grandchildren, rolled around in the middle of them.

She is part of nature. Of course, neither she nor I have to survive the weather. She lives inside, as we do. But she can appreciate and revel in the outdoor world. Actually, I am a part of nature too, animal that I am, with the ability to have wonderful in-body experiences. When I forget that, I have her around to remind me.

If out-of-body experiences exist and are religiously important, I am sure that these in-body experiences are also a path to greater spiritual awareness. God is embodied in the natural world and so are we. The Body and Spirit are one.

There are, of course, significant differences between myself and my dog. We represent different species in the animal world. We can experience some things in the world in similar ways. In other ways, we are worlds apart.

For instance, I love books. You might say I am addicted to them. We have bookcases in almost every room of our big old Victorian house. I read these books. My dog chews them. We devour them differently. The other day I came home and found her in her bed, primly embracing a partially gnawed book entitled,

"Girls are People Too." I don't think my scolding her for almost ruining a book was very effective, punctuated as my words were with my laughter.

Another thing we approach differently is technology. She simply is not into it. It goes right over her head. I have a cell phone, a computer with broadband access, I have a T.V. with a DVD and VCR combo. I have a laptop and a video camera . . . and I am at the low end of the technology spectrum. My dog is not impressed with any of this.

When I sit down to watch T.V. she makes it perfectly clear that she prefers physical interaction. She gently but determinedly tries to distract me by nibbling at my feet or rubbing her toys against my arms and hands or dumping them in my lap.

I have tried to interest her in T.V. to no avail. Well, that's not entirely true: once she heard a barking dog on the screen and turned to check it out. Another time, I rented a video with lots of dogs in it and she actually got interested in it for a minute or two. But there is no doubt about her preferring my undivided attention to watching T.V.

When I work on the computer, she is restless. When I first contemplated getting a dog, I had an image of a sweet pup lying quietly by my side as I worked. What was I thinking?

My dog is simply not plugged in. One of my life goals is notching up her appreciation for, or at least acceptance of, my relationship to technology. I have already made some inroads on introducing her to the pleasure of music. I think she has potential as a dancer. Now to move from a more active to a more passive form of media appreciation.

At the moment, she is making me keenly aware of the fact that a being can have value even without being technologically literate. There is a whole part of our human world that is not wired and has its own integrity. The world of genuine encounter and touch, the world of sense and sight and real community is precious.

I am concerned that the distance between the haves and have-nots in the world of human beings is being defined by ownership of technology. Even as the technological gap narrows, we can remember that human beings in every society are more valuable than the electronic devices they own.

Technology can make great contributions to our lives, to science, to economics, to communications, to medicine, and on and on. It has also brought us more deadly weapons of destruction, more accessible pornography, and violent video games. My dog's simple natural presence reminds me that there is no substitute for affectionate, face-to-face encounter. It will take wisdom, and a lot of advance in human communication, to see to it that we use technology well and value people above our machines.

Dog is on the body side of consciousness and God is on the spiritual side. I am in the middle. We exist in the material and natural world, in the observable universe and interior and transcendent mystical worlds. How can we help but be connected to all of them, to recognize the parts, to pursue harmony between them?

Dog reminds me that contact with the other is beyond technology. I can't reach dog through my wired hook-ups (or wireless either). For real communion I myself must be fully present. I can connect with other human beings through my technological tools, but for some relationships, nothing but real presence will do:

the Martin Buber "I-Thou" reality. It applies to our relationship to nature, to one another, and to God.

My family, my friends, my God, have a right to require of me my full attention, my full being. And I have a right to ask the same of others.

I have strayed a long way from snow. But, in the process, I have been reminded of the fact that in the cold of winter, there is warmth to be found in connection; and in the other seasons, there is pleasure in relationship as well; bodies playing, spirits soaring, life luxuriating, nature moving through its cycles. Joy comes through real connection and communion.

GETTING IT: THE BASICS OF TOGETHERNESS

I N ORDER FOR us to live sane, healthy, productive, peaceable and fulfilling lives together, we all need to make certain adaptations to the people and world around us. This applies to my dog and also to me. We share a household and a community.

I don't make the rules; they are self-evident. We all have to be "housebroken." We can't jump on people and knock them over or push them around. We certainly should not hit, bite or paw each other. We can't play in traffic. We should not litter. The list goes on.

Even though I don't make the rules, I am their instructor and enforcer for my dog, who is new to the world and needs to be introduced to them. Bringing others into social compliance and survival mode makes me sharpen my own behavior and question my own teaching methods.

Trying to educate a pup can be very frustrating. If I thought a dog was going to decrease my stress level and help me live a healthier, happier life, I was wrong – at least in the short term.

Right now, I am stressed to the max. Housebreaking is breaking me. I am forced to try to anticipate my dog's every urge to urinate or defecate so that she learns where to do it. I am also supposed to try to catch her doing it in the wrong place. And she doesn't seem to get it. I have to clean up and I have to listen to my husband complain.

I am tearing my hair out. Actually, once, for two days, she seemed to "get it and do it" in the right place outside. For my part, I seemed to be catching on to her rhythm. She was even "good" over night. But then, she lost it again, just when I was beginning to relax. Are we back to the beginning?

Guided by book upon book, I did not lose it. I did not yell, rub her nose in it, or smack her. I calmly called her attention to her error. She slept in her crate at night, and stayed there when we went out. When she was not contained, we had to dog-proof her environs. She was paper-trained when she came to us. In some ways, that was an asset, but it did mean having to relearn the right place to "go."

When she erred, she was truly sorry. I'm not sure she really knew how she had "sinned." But that she was a sinner – she understood. I hated to see her slink off and look at me with rueful eyes. This is not how it is meant to be.

One day, the upstairs toilet overflowed during the night. When my husband got up, the bathroom was full of water; the water had gone through the ceiling to the two floors below and made an awful mess. Dog was watching him clean it up and sensed his dismay. My husband certainly never blamed her for it; nonetheless, when I came down in the morning she was not her usual effusive self. She had taken this sin upon herself. Water where it does not belong! Distress! It must be me! Goodness!

She not only has to learn how to behave but she also has to learn that everything that goes wrong is not her fault. There are acts of mechanical and human malfunction as well as puppy mistakes – a good lesson for all of us. Some bad things happen that we are not responsible for.

Still, the relationship between dog and me is not great at the moment. I am stressed and she is distraught. All the love that is supposed to flow between us is temporarily blocked by this socialization process, which is not going too well. I still love her. And while I can't speak for her, I think she still cares about me. In any case, we are stuck with each other. I have to trust that she will learn.

In this case, I guess I am god, ruler of her universe. *Top Dog.* They say dogs are pack animals and need a top dog, but I am uncomfortable with the role. I want to be friends. However, there is this matter of living together, and for now, I have to accept the role of educator, if not ruler.

If God feels stress, God must be always and ever strung out, trying to get us to see the things that make for peaceful coexistence. Looking out over Jerusalem made Jesus weep and say, "If only they knew the things that make for peace."

With my dog, as with me and the rest of us, there are good days and bad days, days of lucidity and days of stupidity. Discerning what is best for the survival of our social order, never mind a harmonious life, is sometimes quite self-evident and sometimes elusive in the human realm. Our parents help us with basic socialization but that gets ever more complicated as we become adults. Ethical and just behavior ought to be obvious and natural, but it doesn't seem to be.

No matter how much I care about dog, and no matter how strong and determined I am, I cannot control her physical functions. Eventually she has to get it herself. Since she is a dog, I have to help. I have to make sure she can go outside to do her business. Even if she had a doggy door, I would have to put it there. We are both responsible for a good outcome.

It is quite clear to me that God, no matter how omni-everything, cannot control human beings. God has to wait until we "get it," and stick with us to help us follow through. But no one can live our lives for us. We are, in one way or another, co-responsible with God and one another for our lives and for our world.

Friendship is still hopefully my destiny with dog. And I believe God longs for a mutually responsible relationship with us. There is constant learning that has to go on. Life is an ever-changing kaleidoscope. After we get the basics under control, there is always more.

I think I am going to go play with dog. She needs some cheering up. After all, I think she is trying, and we need to lighten up once in a while. Life can't be all work, and a little fun might enhance our communication and relationship.

I take my religion so seriously. Maybe God would appreciate it if I would lighten up in that arena too. I am sure my God knows how to laugh and play.

APPEARANCE AND ESSENCE

T HE DAY DOG had her first grooming, she got a trim around her eyes. Before the trim, her hair fell perkily over her eyes and she looked very warm and fuzzy, though she probably couldn't see very well. Now her eyes stand out. They are deepset and very dark. Her puppy look is yielding to a more grown-up look. I am disconcerted. I like warm and fuzzy.

My reaction feels much like the one I had when my husband grew a beard. I thought I was living with a stranger, and not one I was sure I liked.

Of course, dog is still herself. I don't think she feels any different but she sure looks different. How strong my reaction is! Visual images are powerful. Same dog. Different look, different identity . . . through my eyes.

How much our images of who God is must affect the way we perceive God. Through my growing-up years and well into my adulthood, I referred to and thought of God in male terms: Father, Son, Lord, King, Ruler, controller of all that is. When those images seem limited and limiting, and I seek new perceptions, God doesn't change just because how I see God changes. But my relationship to God and myself shifts.

I can now imagine God as female and male, as beyond gender, as mystery beyond anyone's naming. God is who God is. I am the one who has to struggle with feelings, visualizations, and words. I now know that using solely male metaphors is idolatrous, denying the fullness of God's essence, making a golden calf of our perceptions of human power. And yet, God as male is so familiar, still seeming somehow warm and fuzzy. What a contradiction!

Where is the Dogness of my dog and the Godness of God beyond my responses and the changing images that catch my mind's eye?

Clearly there is a dog inside the changing visual image of my dog. But my perception of her changes. Of course there are real and not just cosmetic changes going on in her. She is, after all, a dynamic, living creature, growing older each day. But behind these changes is herself, a real living being. I must try to relate to her as she is and as she is becoming. Part of her is still cute and warm beneath those penetrating eyes. And those penetrating eyes were always there beneath the warm and fuzzy. Maybe she is not very complicated. After all, she is a dog. Yet there is intricacy. She is certainly more than a projection of my mind and she has a personality of her own. I have to relate, real person to real dog: a lesson for all my relationships.

On Halloween, we wore wild wigs and scary disguises. Dog was not fooled. I stood in front of her, calling attention to myself. I wanted her to react, but nothing. I could see the wheels turning, "Yeah, what?" She thought I was just the same old me. "Come on," I thought to myself, "surely you are a little put off by my extreme look." Seems not. Then my husband pointed out that she lives by smell and not by sight. Surely that can't be entirely true.

At any rate, dog is not put off by my new look. So much for image and looks in her world! Thank goodness for someone who doesn't care how I look!

The lesson for me is not that looks don't matter at all, but that there is a reality beyond them. How I image God does matter. But all of the imagining and perceiving is, after all, about trying to find the reality or embrace the mystery. Real God. Real me. Real dog. Real granddaughters or grandsons.

We change, but behind the change we are who we are. Our dog, our puppy, is getting bigger. When she was just a little thing and pretty nippy, our youngest granddaughter would give her wide birth. And if she came near her, she would scream. Nonetheless, she was fascinated with her and would call to her when safely behind a screen which the dog would not breach. From that safe haven, she loved to reach out to her and call her name.

Her older sister loved to walk with her and was much more inclined to play with her when she was a few weeks old. Now that she is getting bigger – from fifteen pounds to fifty – our relationships with her are shifting. The younger child leads her around. The older child is more cautious. Dog herself seems very gentle with the younger child and more ready to roughhouse with the older one. She knows who is bigger. When our other older grandchildren come to visit, she has a field day. With them she can romp freely. Relationships shift and depend on the condition or sensitivities of those involved.

I am sure there are many shifts ahead. I like to think we will all come to enjoy each other more and more as we grow together.

I am more watchful of dog now that she is big enough to knock children off their feet inadvertently and annoy adults with her enthusiasm. The thing is, we have lost our cute little puppy and must now appreciate our emerging tween-ager. Someday she will be mature. I hope she keeps her sense of humor and enthusiasm even as I hope she calms down a bit. Even now, there are times when she is very laid back.

We are told that our dog as adult will be much more fun and less work. Right now, we are dealing with an identity crisis. This in-between stage is hard to figure out. What does she need from us now? We just have to go with the flow. Maybe even enjoy the process. My Grandchildren say what dog always needs is hugs and kisses. Maybe we all do!

Process is what life is all about. We are always in some kind of flux. I changed my life when I bought a puppy to see me through a new life change. As she changes, we owe it to each other to work through our transitions.

This leads me to wonder if God changes. I know that when people, or dogs, or other feeling animals are in relationship, change happens as they adapt to each other through evolving life circumstances and events. In a similar way, no matter how constant God is, it seems that God must change too.

My mother was always my mother, but how we related to each other depended on our stage of life, our emotional state, our history and our health, the situation of other family members, the state of the world around us, and our own spiritual development. We both changed.

God is always our God. But as we change, our relationships change us. Love changes us. Love is a verb, as they say, active and dynamic. I like to think that love deepens and strengthens us over time, empowering us, so that as we change we become more truly who we are. So it is that our relationship with God changes too, as we change, and in that sense, God changes.

MY TROUBLE WITH ALPHA DOGS

T HE GOING THEORY is that dogs are pack animals and every dog either is an Alpha Dog or needs one to get them through life. When a dog comes to live with human beings, we have to be the Alpha Dogs.

This is serious business. The dog has to learn to OBEY. This is not just an incident-by-incident matter, but a permanent state of being – for the animal's own good. Just what does this mean? I have read about dreadful, inhumane child-raising techniques, "for their own good." I am searching for another way.

While I agree with the need to be lead-dog until matters such as housebreaking are taken care of and one's pet learns to be a companion and not a nuisance or a danger, and while I know that education is a lifelong undertaking, I found myself having trouble with the concept of being an Alpha Dog for life.

When my husband and I enrolled our dog in a dog training class, I fully expected to learn how to be the ONE IN CHARGE. I was much relieved when I read the following in the *Training Manual* we were given on the first day of class:

> Canine University® educates owners and dogs in a stimulating environment that is relaxed and fun. All of our classes use positive methods that enhance the relationship between owner and dog and because of this we get results!! Leadership is our main goal, since dogs with strong, fair leaders are well behaved, relaxed and do not have behavior problems. We teach you how to achieve this status in a non-violent, non-physical way.

I want our dog to be a companion, a loved and loving member of the household. I really don't have the energy to continually have to assert my Authority. In the beginning, to get the parameters straight, for safety's sake, to help us communicate across our language barrier, and to establish a working and loving relationship, I accept responsibility for training, and (not incidentally) being trained.

From my perspective, if there is an Alpha being in the dog world, it is the trainer who has to help us less-knowledgeable pet companions get where we all want to be.

These trainers are more than willing to give up their role once we, dogs and owners, have graduated from Canine University classes. Our instructor is head of our class pack only temporarily, and once we and our pets understand one another, they move on. There are always more classes we can take, always more to learn. There is always more in any kind of education.

I don't know anything other than the little I have read about dog packs and hierarchies. But I suspect that every member pulls their own weight and has their own personality even when there is a leader.

As a Christian and feminist, I long ago challenged the notion that our human pack needs a sex, or a race, or a culture to lead us. And I didn't have to be religious or a feminist to dislike dictators of all stripes, those over-zealous Alpha Dogs of human systems.

Coming from a working-class background, I am not big on the primacy of one class over another either. Democracy is in my soul. I do not have a need for Top Dogs in my life, nor have I any desire to be one. And I can tell the difference between a Top Dog and a true leader. A true leader has genuine respect for others and uses non-coercive methods to achieve ends. "Leader" is a good word, and I am grateful to those who assume this role in society in a variety of venues.

I was a parent of teen-agers when our society was challenging all authority without always differentiating between types of authority. I was challenging some authority myself and, looking back, I am proud of what we did and who we were in a public sense, taking on injustice, poverty and war as we did in those days. We also explored some personal limitations, and I am left wondering if I could have helped my sons, and myself, to struggle more vigorously with personal boundaries. We could have examined together, more intelligently and in greater depth, the nature of legitimate limits and rightful authority.

I am proud of the men our sons turned out to be and know that they will wrestle with matters of public and private ethics, as fathers in their own time, as I also must continue to do. Being a parent or a leader is always complicated by the need to be able to manage and understand one's own beliefs and behaviors.

The one thing I was always clear about is the value of non-violence in every social sphere of interaction. I was so pleased that when we took our dog for lessons, the trainers we chose turned out to believe in positive reinforcement, rejecting any kind of physical punishment.

As I try to get my dog's attention and work with the reward principle, I am getting somewhere. Of course, I know that certain behaviors cannot be tolerated and my dog needs to get this message. We are fortunate that she is not an aggressive dog. If she were, we would have to curb that behavior.

I wish we could get world leaders to curb their aggressive, self-aggrandizing tendencies. We need to remember that a non-violent approach to life does not imply or suggest that we accept brutal or destructive behavior, but the opposite. It obligates us to resist such leaders.

Not all people or dogs start out on an equal footing. Tough and inhumane circumstances can breed angry and fear-based aggression. Prevention is more effective than addressing problems after the fact. Containment is needed when we fail our responsibilities to one another: containment, employed by just and responsible civil authority.

I cannot imagine that God, who some say has all authority in heaven and on earth, takes pleasure in exercising dominance. That is not what God is about, as I read Scripture. The power of love is at the heart of who God is.

When law is developed to serve the best interests of all, it is an instrument of peace. God's law is given to us to protect us from Top Dogs who think they are above the law and act as a law unto themselves. Breaching just laws developed for the good of all and the rights of minorities causes a breach in social relationship. I want to be in a relationship with my dog that is positive and takes the limits of laws in stride. I limit my impulse to take out my frustration and anger on her, and she responds by trying to please me.

The relationship between God and humanity, like the relationship between humans and dogs, is not one of equality; equality, indeed, is irrelevant. But the desired outcome of our relationship, which is love, requires full acceptance of and respect for the other. In this sense, hierarchy becomes as meaningless and absurd as a winter outfit in the heat of summer.

For human beings, valuing all equally is imaginable and desirable, a first step toward full human rights for all. Beyond equality, however, is freedom to exercise our creativity, make complex ethical choices, and relate to others in agape love, the kind that comes from a spiritual source. In this sense, hierarchy is purely functional, meaningless as an absolute, extremely dangerous when taken too far.

No, I really can't think of God as Top Dog, or King, or Lord: those concepts have such negative connotations for me. They suggest control by force and violence. How could such a God bring us to live peaceably together in the human pack, when the threat of violence is always at the door? Love and dominance are incompatible. God does not share our too-human desire or need for power. We project that on to the Divine. God is God in ways that we cannot begin to fully comprehend, and is there for us in ways that we cannot begin to understand. And, in the Christian community, though equality with God is not something to be grasped by us, we are given the epiphany of God becoming one of us, suffering with us and patiently imparting wisdom so we can become all we are meant to be.

One of the objectives of our dog training class is the development of confidence in our dogs. No tail between their legs for our dogs! We want that for ourselves too.

I am trying to be kind to my dog and she is returning my kindness.

I observed a puzzling thing in our puppy when she was five months old. Confronted by an Alpha Dog who tried to keep her in her place, she was not deterred. Not an Alpha Dog herself, she nonetheless insisted on coming back to test the waters when challenged by an aggressive older dog. In some ways, she was not being too smart. But, in other ways, she showed a great deal of spunk and I admired her. The adults around her had to protect her and temper the other dog's behavior.

In the human realm, the weak need protection from danger and the humiliation of having to submit to unjust or sadistic authority. I have come to the conclusion that kowtowing to aggressive authority is not a natural act, though it may sometimes be a life-preserving one. As much as is possible, we need the spunk to assert our own authority and stand our own ground, the will to help one another curb our worst instincts and practice our best behavior, and the compassion to go out of our way for others.

If we would all attend to the things that make for peace, we would all be more at home in the world. And we can follow those leaders who understand the preciousness of life. Life lessons for dogs and human beings are not all that different.

WIDENING THE CIRCLE

WE HAVE JUST returned from our first long trip with our dog: two days on the road each way, and three days in North Carolina; two days in a motel and three days in the home of our son, daughter-in-law, and two teen-aged grandchildren, and their two-year-old dog.

Our dog was a model traveler. It seems the world is her home. She slept while she was riding in the car – in fact she was so quiet and content that I kept reaching back to see if she was still breathing. To our great relief she had no motion sickness. She never had an "accident" inside anyone else's place, and to our amazement, returned home housebroken. Being on the go and with us almost around the clock worked to socialize our pup!

And, she learned to bark on this trip. Not too much, but just enough to let us know she had her own voice. Her separation anxiety kicked in during the brief times we would leave her alone in the car or in her crate, (the weather being fine for this). She began to "speak" to let us know that she did not appreciate being left behind. Allowing her to have freedom from the crate in the hotel room seemed to work wonders to allay her fears and actually control her barking. For her at least, she needed to feel more in control of her environment. Not all dogs would need that.

She loves people. We are glad to know that she is such a people dog – but found her to be totally undiscerning. She would greet strangers and family alike with the same enthusiasm. She has a lot to learn. Not everyone is trustworthy, or enamored of dogs. Furthermore, how can she be a watchdog if she is not wary of some strangers? On the other hand, how can she continue to enjoy the world if she has to always be on guard? I wonder about that for us humans.

In this age when we are on various stages of terrorism alert in the United States, questions of trust hover over our human heads. And it affects our view of the world and of God. Whom do we dare to love? Is our family our only safe refuge? Is the family itself safe? Are there strangers out there who are as trustworthy as members of the clan, and are there members of the clan who pose some danger? Where is the Holy in all of this? Can God protect us or are we at one another's mercy?

Maybe God can help us discern the times and situations, and at least help us keep our own heads clear. We want to keep our children safe, but we do not want to live by fear or make them inappropriately fearful.

Did I want a companion dog or a watchdog? Can I have both? Can we take care of each other, embrace the stranger, and take reasonable precautions against those who would do harm?

When I was growing up, I lived without fear. I rode to school on public transportation every day. I played in the streets. I fed squirrels in the park with my fingers. I walked home in the dark after a late theater practice, whistling all the way home as I crossed a large empty parking lot and walked down darkened streets. I traveled alone without second thoughts. I felt very secure in my family and relied completely on my father's ability to protect me, and my mother's and grandmother's nurturing presence. I felt safe.

No, I was not fear-free; I had some unrealistic fears placed in my head by a Sunday School teacher and some unthinking family friends. For a while, I was afraid of being in my room at night, even though I shared the room with my sister, and even though I trusted my family and felt at home in the world.

Things have changed. I worry about many things now.

So how do I, how do we, control our own anxieties and still teach our dog to recognize real danger? We don't want to destroy her genuine enthusiasm for life and her love of the world, or our own love of the world. How do we teach our children and grandchildren to be reasonably cautious without losing their spontaneous appreciation of the world?

Will God and my faith protect me from all evil? Or will a simple identification of the enemy as "them," do the trick, dividing the world into an "us" and "them"? Or would such a perspective, rather than making us safe, create an extremely dangerous world?

Sometimes the enemy is within one's self or within one's gates. Our dog could be in as much danger from our mistreating or abandoning her as from some loving stranger. She could be in danger from her own undisciplined behavior. I could do myself in by my own behavior; an addiction, stress, lack of exercise, overwork, you name it. I could love or trust unwisely, or fail to love fully and to trust when it is deserved.

Of course I want to believe that God is my protector. But I know some things are up to me. And I have no easy answers about the balancing of fear and trust. We can begin by following the Scriptural commandment to love God with heart, mind, and soul, and our neighbor as ourselves, or the commandment to love mercy, do justice, and walk humbly with God. But then come the specifics.

Eventually, we all have to learn that some relationships are more trustworthy than others. God is trustworthy, and worshiping other people or material things as though they were ultimate is incompatible with religious integrity and teaching. Anyone who asks for our complete devotion and obedience is suspect. Jesus warned us to be wise as serpents and gentle as doves.

I must confess: I am a jealous pet owner. I want my dog to have a special bond with our family. But I do want her to enjoy others and discern danger.

Our North Carolina family's dog is wonderful: well-trained, loving, and accepting of us as extended family. However, when it came to our dog, he drew the line. He was jealous and wary and territorial. While he did slowly learn to accept her presence, she needed to learn something about boundaries and another dog's space. Their dog needed to know that we could be counted on to protect his interests, and that sharing his space would not lead to the loss of his own place in their family.

Our Maine family has one huge dog, a mastiff, gentle and laid back. It is fun to see our pup and their dog together. That is an easy relationship. When they got two new puppies, she enjoyed them. Our dog is learning to read other dogs, and we need to protect her while she is still naïve.

Life is like that. We have to try to love one another and respect each other's boundaries even as we learn to share. And we have to look out for one another. In the end, we have to accept the fact that not everything is subject to our control, and live as fully as we can anyway. From my faith perspective, even God is not in total control. We have free will as human beings and must accept responsibility for its consequences. And we live with the occasional tumult of nature and the reality of human error and sheer randomness.

There was a time when we, people of all different faiths and faith persuasions, were sure that God was on our side, protecting us and winning our battles for us. In or out of war, we were "the chosen," "the saved," "the righteous ones," the sure-to-be-victorious. I don't think most of us see God as only on our side any more. Of course, it is human to think that our religious perspective is really the "right" one. But then we remember that God loves and watches over all of us.

Not all ways of being together in human community are equally life-giving. We recognize some actions as criminal and rightfully fear those who engage in them. But there are other actions that are criminal in a different way. We need to learn to identify the behaviors that lead more insidiously to the destruction of life: the violent grabbing of privilege and power; the ignoring of the rights of others, the exorbitant feathering of one's own nest at society's expense, and justifying any means to reach ends deemed right or passionately desired. Then we can watch out for those who practice those behaviors, wherever they are; in halls of power or next door, clan members or strangers.

God embraces the whole world. Like our young puppy, we can do that too, but we do not have to do it blindly or naively.

Our dog is a good traveler, albeit with some things to learn about human and animal nature. Her heart is open. Over time, she will become more wary. May her alertness to danger still allow her to keep an open heart.

I want the world to be my home, my children's home, my grandchildren's home and on and on. The truth is that when we travel, we go from one warm home to another. We travel with more than enough food and water. Some people and other creatures of nature don't. The world is their home too. They need what we have and it is up to us to pay attention.

Even traveling with all our needs supplied and a well-behaved puppy, I offered a prayer of gratitude when we returned home safely. It is always good to give thanks for traveling mercies, for the warmth and love of a welcoming family, and for the grace of law-abiding strangers who made our trip pleasant by following the rules of the road and offering genuine hospitality.

We had another traveling experience closer to home. I have already mentioned that we took our dog to Canine University®, about a half-hour away. We, of course, learned more than she did. It was a great experience, being with excellent and kind teachers, other pet owners, and their pups.

I thought, from when we first brought our dog home, that she was beautiful, a wonderful, special dog. The first time I went to puppy class, I learned that everyone else's dog was beautiful, wonderful, special and unique. There wasn't a dog there that I did not like.

The dogs seemed to like being with one another. As in the human community, some dogs were shy, others were outgoing, some wanted to play with toys, others just wanted to romp. Our dog loved running around in circles, artfully jumping over the little dogs, but still making me hold my breath.

The trainer, after observing our dog for several sessions, informed us that she was a "high-energy dog." She loved to run and needed exercise. They didn't say it, but I thought it, "And here she is stuck with two old people." Well, maybe there is a way in which we can be good for each other. But it will take some effort.

I am coming face to face with my own ageism. Suddenly I feel old, when this pup was supposed to make me feel young.

I begin to notice a few things. She is happy if I just stand in one place and kick the ball for her. She can do the running, I can do the planning. When I feel like it, I can run with her. It is fun. I can still move!

I keep waiting for some sign that dog knows how old I am and is ready to make some concessions to age. So far, no acknowledgment has been forthcoming. Can she be so unobservant? I guess so. That's great! She can slow down her pace a little and I can pick mine up.

I notice that the other people in the class are all ages too. There are a few children with their parents. There are grandparents with their children. There are couples and some single adults.

All sizes, colors, and shapes, and they are dressed every which way. The dogs don't seem to care. We should have such a perspective!

In this way, dogs and God have it more together than humans. God shows no partiality and neither, it seems, do these pets.

The wider world has many lessons to teach and we have many lessons to learn, all of us creatures, large and small.

GETTING THROUGH
THE HARD TIMES

I ALWAYS ASSUMED that dog would be a great comfort and distraction when I was feeling down. This did not happen. When the snow turned to ice and the biting cold of the winter truly set in, when a dear friend died, and I finally realized I really was retired and had no place to go each day, and when my husband made it clear that my being around the house was cramping his style, I got depressed. Instead of turning to my dog for relief, I found that I didn't want anything to do with her. I ignored her, which made things worse. Add guilt to my unhappiness.

I don't know if my dog noticed the change in me. She is young and irrepressible. She kept coming around with her toys, wagging tail, and play-with-me stance. All I could do was say, "Not now," or "Go away."

A popular religious assumption is that in our times of trial, God will be there. I am sure God is, but we may not care at such moments. Even God can't always console us when we are feeling down.

Being depressed or grieving can include simply not wanting to reach out to anyone or anything. It can include anger. The reaching out of others to us has to be gentle and persistent.

Dog was not the cure-all I had imagined. That is not her fault. The problem at such times is in us. My dog was no different at that moment in time than at any other time. She was there all along, all of the time. She didn't happen to be at the center of my field of vision. Being down is sometimes turning off and being wrapped up in one's own hurt, having to live through it in order to heal.

Mercifully, my descent into misery didn't last. Not that each of the issues got resolved like magic or that I wouldn't experience such a time again. My grief was still strong and I missed my friend, but I knew he would want me to go on with my life. And I wanted some sign that he was in a better place.

I tried to fill my time with creative work. As for my husband and me, we are learning to share the same space. Change is hard and retirement is a huge change that we are coping with. Ultimately, we hope to appreciate and enjoy it! And I am back to acknowledging my dog's existence and finding some pleasure in her company.

Soon enough, my dog's time came to undergo her own challenge. The veterinarian suggested that she be spayed. In addition to the impending surgery, she had an ear infection, and was seriously in need of a bath just when she couldn't have one.

She did well with the surgery, sailed right through it, and wasn't half as effected as I was – that is, if you look at emotional factors as well as physical ones. She was, after all, the one who was spayed and could never have puppies. I wistfully asked the receptionist at the animal hospital if this procedure could be reversed. The answer was a definitive "no."

Everyone acted as if the decision to spay her was almost a given, the clear thing to do. "Too many dogs in the world already. Better for her health, and prevents certain cancers." But she is special and has a pedigree. Maybe there should be more of her in the world.

I am a female just as she is and I was thinking about how important my reproductive system is to me. Eventually I was able to distinguish between my dog and myself and to remember that for some of my friends who had had a hysterectomy, and for all of us who are aging and leaving our reproductive years behind, it is not the end of the world or of our being whole people.

"Don't fool with mother nature." Sometimes Mother Nature benefits from intervention. Or is it Father Nature? Mother God, Father God. Mother Nature, Father Nature. Mother Time, Father Time. Whatever.

It is done and she is fine and I am in recovery, from all that came before, and from this latest crisis. I am more resilient than I may seem when I am feeling down. Maybe some of the way she takes life in stride will rub off on me and I will learn to flow more easily with the inevitable up and down of life.

On the other end of nature and finitude is God, with the view of eternity. Maybe Divine transcendence and perspective can rub off on me too. I am part of an ageless continuum of creation, in and beyond our world, reproductive or not!

Today the sun is out and I am in a good mood. Because of her surgery, dog cannot go outside and play. But she can take a walk. Maybe we can brave the ice and snow to do that. Dog generates some energy around me, and the affection she shows is now healing for me.

God is energy too, and affection. What bothers me is that I seem to have to work so hard to tap into that energy and love. I would like to just throw myself on those Everlasting Arms, on someone else, on anything else to take care of everything when I am tired and depleted. I can see it now. I was grieving and I was tired.

But it didn't seem as if I could afford to rest. I felt as if I had to take care of myself and others too. I needed to learn to let go more. Meditate. Open myself to Divine mercy and healing!

Mind over matter, they say. My mind could do without the responsibility for matter, for physical things; in fact, my brain is one of those physical things, part of my body after all. I have been attending to my dog's physical needs. It is good to take care of my own too. I owe my body. It has served me well. But sometimes my body has to fend for itself!

The thing about animals, other than humans, is that they remind us of the physicality of life. There is spirit there too, of course. Perhaps wherever there is life there is spirit. But with my dog, it is hard to know where the mind part comes in, the consciousness. Consciousness seems eclipsed by instinct. Do we underplay the centrality of instinct in ourselves? the critical place that meeting our basic needs plays in our own lives? Deny instinct, and the pursuit of it can take over. I would like to be more natural, more in tune with nature.

I wonder if my temporary depression came partly from physical deprivation, from the coming of the cold, the diminishing of the light, the need to be nurtured as well as to nurture?

God is not going to take winter away, or nurture us with an empathetic touch. God can reach out to our hearts, cajoling us to serve one another and preserve one another in the winter times of life. God's good energy surrounds us. It is ours for the harnessing. If we look around and are willing to receive, there is also the positive energy of others to buoy us up.

I think part of me is still depressed, not in a personal way, but over the state of the world and the violence that seems to be everywhere. My granddaughter said to me the other day, "We are at war, aren't we?" I said that we are in a war in Iraq. Then I turn on the television and listen to the rhetoric about the "War on Terrorism." Are we in an all out war, or inventing one? It seems as if we are drumming up fear by creating and speaking of the concept of war. Why? Why can't we talk about "Containing Terrorism," or even "Combating Terrorism," or "Preventing Terrorism?" If we play with the concept of War it will come home to haunt us. We will invite it. We will goad others into it.

War is so much the opposite of creativity and caring for one another.

People used to think that God got involved in war, choosing sides. Most of us are changing our perceptions of God . . . and of holy wars. There has to be another way to deal with human evil. Fighting evil with evil is dangerous and destructive business. All war is unholy.

War is a human invention, as far as I know. Animals other than humans have power struggles, sometimes to the death. They have to worry about predators and natural disasters. Some experts believe that wild animals escaped the destruction of the last awful, destructive Tsunami because they sensed it coming and got out of the way. Mostly, I think, when most animals face life-threatening situations, they prefer to get out of the way.

I so want to get out of the way of war. I am sure that my dog is a peaceful creature. She is a hunting dog by breed, but she is not hunting now. (She continues to chase squirrels, but they always get away!) She doesn't even like it when people argue around her. My sister's dog, who lives on a farm, did catch a chicken when we were there. But she brought it to them as a trophy, it was a prize for the humans.

The question is, "Who are we humans?" The future is in our hands. So much is left to us to handle. We are in desperate need of the Wisdom that can lead us in paths of peace.

Once again I am reminded that God cannot "fix" things without us. Sometimes that feels overwhelming and sometimes we each need a "time out" from worry. But Wisdom is there, capable of calling our spirits to full strength so we can function in the midst of all the swirling events around us, and be with one another in love as we are meant to be, dog included. We are not put in this world to conquer life, or compete with one another for sustenance. We are here to share life's blessings, to organize life for the good of all, to enjoy its bounty, and appreciate life's beauty, and the simple things.

There are times when a feeling of depression or depletion or grief catches up with me. But ultimately, I want to believe that people, including myself, are good, albeit flawed. And I know my dog is wonderful and God is good.

LEAVE IT!

T HERE IS A lesson we have in dog class called "Leave it." We practice this concept in many different ways. First we put some treats on the floor in front of our dog, who is quietly lying there, and tell her or him, "Leave it." And they learn. Later, we toss some food on the floor with the same command. Next we do our heeling exercise and walk past plates of food on chairs which they must learn not to touch. Finally, as we walk in a circle with our dogs, if they move inappropriately toward another dog, we tell them, once again, "Leave it!"

At home, I am challenged to use this command, to tell dog, who obsesses over squirrels, "Leave them." This is not easy for her to do. In fact, up until now, it is impossible. When she sees a squirrel, she goes into high alert. If I am on the other end of a

57

leash, she is strong enough to pull me along or knock me over as she darts with utter singleness of purpose after the small animal. If she is inside looking out the window, her whole body shakes, she pants and runs from window to window. The best I can do so far is remove her from the stimuli.

What, I wonder, am I going to do if we are dealing with a life-long addiction/obsession? I can work on the "Leave it" exercises. What I can't do is leave her. I am committed to (read "Stuck with") this DOG!

If a person is destructively addicted, a serious sexual offender, for instance, removal from society by imprisonment may be the only option. If a person is abusive in a particular situation, then separation is the only safe path when other options have been explored.

With my dog, behaviors like chasing squirrels, while utterly frustrating, are not (usually!) harmful, and come from her being of the canine species. She and I are both animals, different but not equal, each with our own obsessions to overcome. We have to work together on a manageable compromise between her nature and our own.

In the human realm, we sometimes hear that phrase, "different but equal." In that context it is almost always shorthand for some kind of discrimination, an excuse for dividing people into groups that are indeed different but definitely not equal.

With my dog, our being different and not equal is all right. She is not worrying about categories, about justice or injustice.

My relationship with God is not equal and we are different and that is also all right, and important to remember. I may be in God's image, but so too are all other human beings, I am one among many. And while we humans are in this world, we live in a different domain from God.

God is mystery. Even though, from a Christian perspective, God has been revealed to us, and even became one of us in Jesus Christ, we see through a glass darkly, as the Apostle Paul said we do. Humanity may be created in God's image, but we are beings in process, becoming who we are meant to be. And that only happens in communion with one another, since it takes all of humanity to truly reflect the wholeness and complexity of God's image. Even then, in our finite state, we cannot embrace the fullness of Divine transcendence.

However, the message through the ages is that God and humanity are in relationship. We are stuck with one another, so to speak – that is, if God exists, and I choose to live as if God does. I have had glimpses of God that touch my heart, and lead me to faith. Sometimes those glimpses are direct, sometimes through other people, sometimes through Scripture, sometimes through nature, art and science, sometimes even through dog. But I digress.

My subject is "Leave it." To some extent, I have to learn along with my dog: there are times when I must "Leave it." For instance, with food, there are some things I should not eat. I like food as much as my dog does. I can even bribe myself with treats. When I have had a hard day, I need a piece of chocolate. And at night when I am tired and relaxing, why not a snack? A really good one?

"Leave it!"

Addictions and obsessions are part of our human life. Money is a great tempter. Worry is another. Alcohol, drugs, sexual obsessions, material things, gambling, "Leave them!" Whatever becomes an idol, leave it. Whatever tempts you to harm another, leave it. Whatever leads to addiction, leave it.

I simplify. But there is much to be learned and gained from this part of my dog's training. The thing is, I am helping my dog with this life lesson. Now, who or what will help me? Maybe in a way, she is already helping me by my having to reflect on teaching her.

Squirrels and food are not the only problem for my dog. She needs to leave other dogs alone some of the time, and some dogs all the time. Just as my dog needs to learn these lessons, I do too. I need to learn to leave some people alone all the time and all people some of the time. As much as I am admonished to love everyone, that does not mean that I get along with everyone. There are some people with whom I cannot have a mutually satisfying relationship. Some people may be a bad influence in my life, or abusive. Still others may be very tempting but off limits.

God loves everyone. As a religious professional, I try to reach out to everyone. But if I am honest, I cannot: I am not God. I have to respect my own vulnerabilities and limitations. I have to recognize the problems or personalities in other people that may be downright harmful to me. If I try unrealistically to do good for everyone, it will keep me from doing the good that I can do.

Sometimes we can see relationships coming that we need to avoid, and sometimes we can't. What I have come to understand is that God does not require me to tolerate all kinds of behavior. In fact, God is as actively trying to teach me the "Leave it" command as I am actively trying to teach it to my dog.

But what about forgiveness? That is a kind of "leave it" command, too. They say that dogs do not hold a grudge. But I think they do remember. What about us? Can we leave the past, and forgive, and move on?

The reasons we are learning to teach our dogs the "Leave it" command is so that they can live out the fullness of their days. If a dog eats every morsel it finds on the ground, it could end up very sick. If a dog blindly chases a squirrel across the lawn and into the street, it can get killed. If a dog does not learn to turn away, if it possibly can, from an aggressive dog when being attacked, it could be seriously hurt or even killed.

Forgiveness, of course, is not connected to enduring or engaging in ongoing, unsafe behavior. Leaving danger behind is essential to survival. Forgiveness is what happens when we look back from a safe place, at an incident, a war, or a trauma of any kind, which is over.

Each day may be new to my dog. But I am sure that dogs carry the memory of abuse in their bodies. If they have a chance, and if they are still able, forgiveness for them must mean being able to trust again, moving on. Keeping on.

Dogs don't have the complex consciousness that people have. For us, forgiveness is complicated and hard. Part of forgiveness is coming to terms with our own imperfections, without blaming ourselves for the behavior of others. Part of forgiveness comes with the sure knowledge that revenge accomplishes nothing. Who knows but that there but for the grace of God go I? – or there but for the grace of upbringing, of context, of history, of biology, of whatever.

Forgiveness is easier in the context of God who is our final judge. Ultimate knowing is not in our hands. And, if we can understand that God is merciful with us, ought we not to show mercy to others? We too have been offenders in our lifetime. As it says in Scripture, "All have sinned."

We have our laws, our court systems, our human judgments. These are essential. But when our human systems have run their course, many are guilty of crimes against humanity who will never be identified or prosecuted. Justice is not always done. Yet we all have to get on with life. Leave it, and get back to living.

COMMUNICATION: THE LANGUAGE OF THE HEART

COMMUNICATION BETWEEN PEOPLE of the same species is hard enough without throwing in communication with a totally different species. Language is so important. Human beings speak many different tongues, but we all rely on words.

My daughter-in-law had been going deaf since late childhood; so she and my son and their daughters began to learn sign language. We began to pick up a few words too. Communicating words with their hands and facial expressions was essential to their being a family and to our connecting with them. She now has a cochlear implant and her hearing is much improved. But exploring a new kind of language, a more physical language, has added a new dimension to life.

The thing about dog is that she does not speak any language. She can learn hand signals and over time will learn some words. But unless I learn to read her body language and she begins to express herself more clearly, she will have trouble "speaking" to me. So far this does not bother her; I am the only one frustrated by it.

We need to understand one another's emotions and needs. Whereas in the beginning we just needed touch, the pat here and the nibble there, now we need more complex interaction. How do we reach across our species divide?

I watched a program on television about dogs performing heroic rescue missions: dogs that were not trained for this, but did it spontaneously. Amazingly, a blind dog was able to rescue a swimmer in trouble. The other day I stepped in some deep snow and had trouble getting up. My dog wagged her tail and licked my face and thought we were playing. Would she know what to do if I were really in distress? If I began to freeze there on the spot? I feel a need to get our signals straight.

I have read about how Native Americans could communicate with animals. They could connect in some language beyond words. I have seen movies about it too. And there was Tarzan, who was raised by apes, who learned to interact with his adopted family in a unique way. Non-verbal connection, real intimacy.

If communicating with the animal world is difficult, what about communicating with a Divine being? Mystics of all religions experience this transcendent connection. But for most of us, this is not easy, even though many of us pray and meditate.

Sometimes it seems that direct encounter with the Holy is for prophets and religious leaders. They are the ones whose stories are set down in words, in Scriptures and other holy writings, who record revelation from another realm. Or does God communicate directly with ordinary people? And if so, how?

Dog is of course real, verifiable, even if our mode of communication is not always clear. But God's reality is not visible, and therefore the very existence of God is open to question. When it comes to the Holy, not only do we have to ask about the language we use, but whether or not there is anyone or anything there with whom to speak. Communication outside of one's own species is hard to come by, and takes a concerted effort. And communication with the unseen is truly a matter of faith.

I can assume that my dog wants to communicate with me. Her life depends upon it and her affectionate nature requires love. Forgive me if I draw a parallel with my relationship to God. I believe in a Divine Reality wanting to communicate with us human beings, for sheer love of us.

My assumption that there is a God is based on three things. One is simply that I know there is a reality, an energy beyond what our senses can fathom or measure, a soul-life dimension, something invisible, beyond us, in us, between us, and around us. The second is the testimony of women and men through the ages as recorded in Holy Writ and other inspired writings. Their witness rings true for me. And finally, I believe I can communicate with God in my own tongue, even if it is, as the Apostle Paul says, "with sighs too deep for words."

At times, I feel God's closeness to me as the rock beneath my being, and the light within. I have also seen God in the faces of others and felt God in human embrace.

Sometimes communicating with God or nature seems easier than communicating with members of my own species. Real communication with our own kind or with other beings, animal or Divine, is best described, I think, as the language of the heart, the language of love.

Love is a complicated emotion which is sometimes returned, sometimes betrayed, sometimes fully appreciated, and sometimes misunderstood; sometimes frustrated, and sometimes fulfilled. Love can also be confused with infatuations and superficial attachments.

My dog seems very loving when she is around me but she is as fickle as she can be when anyone else is near. She goes leaping and straining for their attention. Of course I want her to be friendly with others, to love other members of our family, to be appropriately affectionate with friends, but at the same time to save some special affection for me.

Loyalty, that's what I want. I want a lot from her. I want her to be my dog, but I also want her to be enough at home with others to do well when I must be away from her.

I have counseled enough couples and examined my own life enough to know that straying from the straight path of loyalty is a very universal human problem. Of course no relationship can be all things to any person. We all need colleagues and friends as well as significant others to complete our lives. However, marriage needs to be a protected relationship and more intimate than all others to have any meaning beyond its legal status. We cannot escape the issue of boundaries.

In one of the Ten Commandments, God is described as a jealous God, wanting us to have no other gods. We will have other interests and loves alongside our relationship to God. The commandment is about not turning anyone or anything else in life into an ultimate loyalty.

I confess that I am as distractible and disloyal as my dog is with me, when it comes to my relationship with the Holy One. I know I am not called to a monastic life of total devotion. How then to keep my priorities straight in the midst of my fairly frenetic life? If I believe in the value of communication with a Beloved Other, a communication of the heart, I have to leave time for it and pay attention for it. And I have to know that God is delighted with and in our human loving which needs time and attention too.

My husband says we do not spend enough time with our dog, doing her training exercises and playing with her. Still we are trying to please one another and wanting to live together in harmony. Time and energy, that's what matters of the heart require.

I probably don't need to worry about my dog rescuing me when I have fallen through the ice, or am frozen in snow (to return to my opening thoughts), but I do need my dog not to pull me down icy steps or take off after a squirrel when I am on the other end of the leash. I would like her to be street smart, and always come when she is called, just to protect her from danger. I know she needs me to give her an outlet for her energy as much as she needs limits set. Some things are simple matters, no-brainers when it comes to communicating love.

And then there is heart talk that has nothing to do with security and safety, or exercise, but more with pleasure and making one another smile. We can do that for one another, dog and me. We may not speak a common language, but we are not total strangers to one another, sharing a common household as we do and having our own spirit bond.

I appreciate a religious message that appears in many faiths: the whole world is God's Household, and all of us, creatures large and small, share it in common. We need more heart talk both for survival and the things that give us joy.

One more thought. We communicate by touch and not just by words; the good kind of touch, shared appropriately, which caresses and cares for, which is essential to nurturing the life force, which provides healing and comfort, which delights and brings pleasure.

I can share and enjoy touch with my dog. I cannot physically touch the Divine. For the divine touch we are given to one another in human families and communities. And we are given the companionship of other animal species. We can exchange nurturance. We can feel with one another. We can exchange loyalties. We can make one another laugh.

Communications of the heart.

REAL CHANGE

WHERE DO I begin? My dog went to the groomer yesterday. She has been there before and I have written about it before. But this time was different, a real shocker. She went in looking like a big, white, fluffy lamb, lovable, puppyish, beautiful. She came out looking like a skinny, denuded creature, with scrawny legs that seemed barely able to hold her body up. I recognized her face on one end and her puff of a tail on the other. As far as looks go, she was now a dog much harder to love!

My granddaughter, who went with me to pick her up, was very good about it. She treated her as she always had, reached out to her as the wonderful dog she is, and basically ignored the change. But I was obsessed by it, aware that my feelings for her had changed. This was a dog that was not going to get away with everything.

This was a dog I could distance myself from. This was a dog . . . this was still my dog, still the same dog, but . . . I was feeling as if I needed a change too, a big attitude change.

I think dog knew that she was different. She seemed to be more subdued, had a different, more self-conscious sense of herself. Maybe she was feeling as bare and denuded as she looked.

I thought the whole thing was my fault because I had allowed her long hair to become matted. They told me they would have to take her hair down to an inch or an inch and a half. But less than a quarter of an inch! Maybe I should have been angry. She looked awful. I felt guilty.

Change. Real change. I have already written about essence and change but here it was in bold relief! Maybe human beings change that much, several pounds up and down. Graying hair, or a variety of hair colors. Aging: adolescence, old age. But except for hair color, big changes don't happen overnight, or in a few hours. Though I suppose they could; a fire, an accident, an illness. This was DRAMATIC!

I couldn't help but wonder again about changing and God. If God loses some of the traditional characteristics we always assumed God to have, can we accept God in her/his new representation?

My dog seems so vulnerable now. And much smaller. That leaves me feeling much bigger and more in charge and somehow, more detached. Not what I bargained for when I took her for a grooming.

She is lying beside me now. One good thing about the hair removal is that she is much softer. Not the kind of soft that you can rub your hands through and ruffle up, but soft like velvet. Underneath the velvet she is hard, bony and muscular. The shape of her body is clear and hound-like. I want to feed her more. I want to get her back to her old self . . . or rather, to my preferable image of her.

I have to take her for a walk. I was always proud to be with her, she was so cute and people stopped to look at her. Now she is scrawny and I am ashamed of her. People will wonder what kind of waif she is and how she has been mistreated. I dread the next visit to the vet.

Then she pulls ahead. I become aware of how strong she is. In that department, she is her old self. With or without the fur, she is strong, not as frail as she seemed when shaved practically to the bone. Appearances can indeed be deceiving.

I am going to have to get over it. The hair will grow back and both she and I will have to make it through the discipline of brushing. Now I know my dog is a poodle. She looked like a hairy sheep dog before, or maybe more like the ideal dog I dreamed about. My Dreamy.

She is actually growing into herself. The groomer says I have a high maintenance dog. If so, I will have to learn something about maintenance.

Good grief! How hard it is to love someone for who they are. My husband, who had a negative, frou-frou image of a poodle, kept assuring everyone that while our dog was indeed a poodle, she would never have to look like one. Of course, what he meant was, she would not have to have a typical poodle cut. What I didn't realize was that we both had some resistance to her actually looking like herself, fancy hairdo or not.

The fact is, she will have to look like herself. I, we, will have to get over our ridiculous feelings about image, and will have to love her as she is, whatever that happens to be. That does not mean that we won't be working on our behaviors or appearance, her training and ours. It does mean that she is going to be who she is, and that cannot be defined by me.

Funny, I thought I knew that. But when confronted with it in real time and space, again, as if for the first time, I was thrown for a loop. When I saw who my dog is underneath all the warm fuzzies, I freaked. I really did.

So much for warm fuzzies. Getting to the real person, the real dog, or true God, is not ever as easy as having to cope with a haircut. But there it is, one of life's hardest and most rewarding tasks, loving the other as they are. I suppose the corollary to that is learning to be who we really are, and facing the truth about ourselves. For a while there, I was loving an image. Probably not the first time in my life!

My granddaughter had it right. She is still young enough to be gentle and see through facades. I, on the other hand, have to peel off the armor of years, and get back to basics. My head is full of ideal images by now: concepts of perfection and deception, expectations and imaginings. How can I ever appreciate what is true, real, and transparent?

I am sure there are still many lessons lying ahead in the journey with my dog and the rest of my family, and in my spiritual pilgrimage. My dog just gave me a look that would melt anyone's heart and brought a toy for me to play with. It is time to stop typing for now and show a little more love for my real dog, the one inside the fur, long or short.

HAPPY BIRTHDAY

DOG IS NOW one year old. With our grandchildren we celebrated her birthday. In place of the traditional chocolate cake that marks many birthdays in our families, we had special bones and a little vanilla ice cream (chocolate is bad for dogs). We put a ribbon in her hair (which came out immediately) and sang to her. We could have sung, "You've come a long way baby," but we serenaded her with the usual "Happy Birthday."

Dog is still very young, with more energy than I have by a long stretch, but she is truly sweet and an important part of our family, and she is growing up! She, we, have learned so much.

Of course, there are still some rough edges. Now that she is over sixty pounds, jumping on people is really out, pulling on the leash when I take her for a walk is a drag, and she could be better about coming when she is called.

We all learn to exchange some independent behaviors to get along with one another. The world around all of us is wonderful and full of marvels. It is also full of hazards, as noted earlier. We negotiate the challenges as best we can and enjoy the wonders.

As she celebrates her birthday, we are having a good time with her and we are back to the old battle of wills, as we move through our various transitions together.

We all benefit from our daily learning of mutual give and take.

Of one thing I am sure, I certainly do not want to break my dog's spirit. I love the spirited side of her, even the stubbornness she exhibits when she puts on the brakes and says simply, "I do not want to do that." How else can she let me know what she wants? But we have to continue to negotiate the rules and each other's needs.

When rules are just and fair, they provide us with survival skills that hold us from the brink of chaos and order our world. Our own survival rules are different from this dog's and even more important to learn. The laws which support individual growth and the development of community grow out of our needs, some essential, some deeply desired, and some optional.

At this milestone in her life, we and our dog are back in class at Canine University. I am taught that the key to helping us both learn is getting her attention. It is not treats, though they are important; it is not punishment, which does not work over the long haul. It is getting her to look at my eyes.

"Look at me," I say. Eventually, over time, she begins to check in with me. She has to modify her own behavior. I can't do it for her, but I can and will do everything within my power to get her attention so we can inhabit, explore and enjoy the world together. I can help her shape her behavior for a long and happy life while she teaches me to see things in new ways.

Left to her own devices, she would chase squirrels all day. And they would enjoy tormenting her, peering down at this large creature barking and acting like an idiot, from their safe and superior place on a high tree limb. Left to my own devices, who knows what obsessions I would chase after?

I obviously cannot change her being a dog anymore than I can change my being a human being, nor would I want to. But I can help her channel her doggy ways and try to channel my human nature. We live in the midst of an urban environment where everyone deserves and needs the give and take of reciprocal respect. But not everyone gets or gives that respect. Sometimes it seems like everyone is just looking out for themselves.

I think about God and ethical behavior in human beings; the importance of being trustworthy, of caring about other people, the value of integrity and the significance of self-control.

God cannot live my life or anyone else's for us. Just as my dog has to learn her own lessons, I do too. Education is a lifelong process for which there is no substitute.

I learned a great deal about myself when I discovered that the key to bonding with my dog in a positive way is getting her to look into my eyes. Attentiveness, listening, connecting, asking, responding – these are at the heart of my relationships with all creation and with God. God is not out to break my spirit, or enslave me. God values my independence, but is wise enough to lead me to practice my gifts in the context of trustworthy interdependence.

Everything is interconnected in this world. Interdependence, it seems to me, is a given, not a choice. In the daily living of our lives we constantly have to make decisions that either impede or contribute to Life, living with one another in ways that protect and enhance, or destroy and cheapen.

Those of us who can make those decisions are the lucky ones. For some people and other life forms, the struggle for survival obliterates all else.

Far too many children, never mind canines, feel alone or are alone in the world. There is no opportunity for mutuality, no one to look them in the eye with compassion and understanding. No one even trying to get their attention. God is there for them, but where there are no human beings to mediate God's presence, how can they know about it, let alone believe in it? That is when they are ripe for ideologies based on dominance and violence.

The thing about the Holy One, is that s/he relies on us to mediate love, to introduce one another to "the things that make for life." The teachers at Canine University send us home each week to practice our lessons. We all need to practice living hospitably in the world.

When we look into the eyes of God, that is a step toward rediscovering the good that creation can be.

You might say that this second round of classes was our dog's birthday present. During the time that she was in class, when we learned about how important it is to look in one another's eyes, we learned how important we are to one another and how promising the future is. That made our birthday celebration really happy.

Dog came down with her first illness right after we celebrated her birthday, in the middle of class sessions. Even though she had

had her shots for kennel cough, she came down with a severe case of it. It happened the week that we were due to visit our grandchildren in Maine whom we had not seen for a long time.

Thus, in our dog's second year, we opened a new chapter in our lives together, the chapter of truly sharing the care of our dog. I had gone through this as a parent with our children. Once I got over feeling that I had to be everything for them, omnipresent with them, and in total control, I was able to be realistic and share their care with others. Of course, my husband and I always remained responsible for parenting and overseeing all of their care.

With dog's illness, the first person we leaned on was our Veterinarian. He was helpful and reassuring and prescribed the medicine dog needed. We started her on her meds and then had to decide what to do about our trip to Maine. Taking the dog along, or putting her in a kennel, was not an option (she was contagious).

We could call off our trip but it would be a long time before their schedules and ours would make a visit possible.

Could she stay at home? A dear friend was staying at the house who has had dogs of his own. "Sure," he said. He would take care of her in the evenings and let her out in the morning; she could sleep in his room. But during the day, his daughter needed him. Our son agreed to take care of her over the dinner hour. Even with all this help, she would be alone all day! I worried.

Still, we chose to go to Maine. Our grandchildren and their parents were our priority. We had a reasonable way to provide for dog's care. Leaning on our friend and our son, with the veterinarian as a back-up, off we went. Even though everyone assured me that our dog would be fine, I was anxious. It was a familiar feeling. Often in life we have to make hard choices, and we make them as best we can, and live with the uneasiness they create.

We had a good time in Maine on the evening we spent there. But when the next day came, I felt we had to get back as early as we reasonably could, allowing for some quality time with our grandchildren. Whenever I see the words "quality time," I am looking at a short-hand way of saying "When time has to be divided between competing claims, the one getting Quality Time comes out on top."

I found myself trying to imagine the stress put on a God who has to juggle billions of competing claims. Didn't Jesus say that even the hairs of our head are counted by God? Clearly Jesus was not being literal. He was using exaggeration to make the point that every human life is precious to God.

This is, I confess, beyond my grasp. God's being is beyond my comprehension, let alone the vastness and inclusiveness of God's love. Still, what I take away from these thoughts is the fact that not one of us is more important than any other from a Divine perspective. The Vet taking care of our dog takes care of many other dogs, our son who helped out has his own family and friends, our friend helping us out has his daughter and his own priorities. You get the point. I would like to think sometimes that I am unique in God's eyes, and so I believe myself to be, but so also is everyone else. And that is, somehow, very comforting and reassuring.

Well, dog survived our absence, but it wasn't all ideal. The not-picture-perfect part while we were gone included her having two peeing accidents and some coughing fits. When we got home, she was not fine, she was at the peak of her kennel cough (which she would have been even if we had stayed home).

We needed a midnight consultation with the Vet, who responded quickly. To our panicked, "She's choking!" he gave us a reassuring solution that worked. We took her in the bathroom and ran the hot water in the shower, creating a steam room, just as we had done when our children had croup. It worked with the dog as it had worked with them. Having this dog is almost like having a child . . . . or maybe an alter ego. Certainly it is safer to allow a dog to become an alter ego than a child.

Hilary Clinton says it takes a village to raise a child. Well, it takes a whole network to raise a dog, too. And a whole community to support me. Without doctors I would not be alive today. Without my parents' love and caring for me, I would have shriveled up and died. Without my teachers I would not be educated. Without my church, I would not have embraced religion or entered the career in ministry that I have loved. Without my family and network of friends, I would not know the depths and challenges of love.

I wonder, does God ever need community and caring for?

Jesus said that if we take care of one another, it is like taking care of Jesus himself. How God, the universal life force, must suffer when we are in pain, or sick, or suffering, or lashing out at one another! If we don't take care of one another, God suffers, the world is out of balance. For restoring the world, we have each other and the energy of Divine love.

If I thought that having a dog would lengthen my life, I was dreaming. She may have cost me a few years through the worrying I have done, for all I know. But then, love makes life worthwhile even when it is costly. In some ways, dog has limited my freedom as people said she would. But life is much richer with her. She is a good companion, her approach to the world is refreshing, and she brings me happiness. She is always ready for an adventure and now that she looks me in the eye, we are ready to go places.

If I wanted to, I could say that life without God would be easier too. God can be demanding. But, God, though a trustworthy presence, is more than a good companion; God is the ground of my being. God also knows how to laugh and bring happiness, and when I look in the mysterious eyes of God, I see a twinkle. In God's presence, I understand more about myself and my world. God is love, and I am in love with life.

Now life includes my dog, and I am very grateful for her. Happy Birthday, my faithful companion, and many more!

Made in the USA
Middletown, DE
01 May 2016